How to Discover Your Purpose in Life in 30 days Workbook

Edited by Bishop C.L. Green MTh, DD, Zadie Glenn-Francis
Cover Design and Graphics: Blessing Theophilus-Israel

Dedicated to Jesus Christ, my Lord and Saviour who gave me the inspiration to write this book.

Table of Contents

Introduction

Dear Reader, welcome!

Purpose is a subject that is close to my heart because just about five years ago I did not know what my purpose was in life. I was living a frustrated and defeated life, until I heard a message that changed my life. The message was given by Apostle Alfred Craig and the message was that you will know you are living on purpose when you love what you are doing and wake up every day feeling excited about what you are doing.

At that time in my life, I was not living an exciting life, and I knew from my Christian background that I could not find my purpose outside of God, therefore I totally surrendered my life to Jesus Christ who is the Way to the Father and then asked Him to show me God's purpose for my life.

I asked this question consistently for 30 days and at the end of the 30 days God spoke. He gave me a dream which revealed to me my purpose and because the dream was too great for me to fathom, I asked Him that if it truly was from Him, He should confirm it. He did, and I had the same dream two weeks after.

Ever since that day, my life has never been the same. I am now living my life everyday on purpose and God has gifted me with the ability to create this workbook to help you to discover your purpose in life in 30 days, just like I did.

If you will follow the exercises faithfully, I am certain that you will discover your purpose in life in 30 days.

It is my prayer that this workbook will empower you to discover your purpose in life and to guide you to reach your full potential.

With love,
Blessing Theophilus-Israel

What is Purpose?

There is a purpose or reason for everything. The purpose of a microwave is to heat food. The purpose of a car is to take you from one destination to another. Everything has a purpose. Purpose is God's original intention for you, it is the reason why God created you. Do you know the reason why you were born?

In life we create value by the problems we are willing to solve. What specific problem were you born to solve? What is your assignment in life?

I want to assure you that there is a reason why you are alive, and your responsibility is to find out what that is. Sadly, many people are alive but they are not really living. They are what you may call the walking dead. Many people have been born and have died without ever discovering why they were born or what they were created to do. You are alive, but what are you meant to do? Each one of us has been called and given a specific purpose, even before time began:

Who has saved us and called us with a holy calling, not according to our works, but according to His own purpose and grace which was given to us in Christ Jesus before time began
2 Timothy 1:9

I am certain that you cannot really begin to live until you know the specific reason why you are here and what problem you have been born to solve. For you, reader, as you hold this App / workbook in your hand, be assured that this will not be the case for you.

Discovering your Identity

If you can answer the questions below then you are well on your way to discovering your purpose in life.

1.   Who am I? (How would you describe yourself?)

....
....
....
....
....

2.   What am I passionate about?

....
....
....
....
....

3. What am I naturally good at? (i.e. gifts, talents and skills)

....
....
....
....
....

4. What would you like to do if I had all the time, skills and resources?

....
....
....
....

5. What would I like to change in the world if I could?

....
....
....
....
....

6. Why do I think I have been created?

....
....
....
....
....

7. What would I like the world to remember me by?

....
....

If answering these questions, has taken you time, it is perfectly fine. If you had difficulties answering the questions above, please do not give up. Persevere and by the time you get through this app, go back to the questions and you will find it much easier to answer them.

1. **Do I believe in God?**

Yes – move to 30-day challenge
No – answer the questions below:

2. **Why don't I believe in God?**
   o Parental upbringing?
   o Science, books on evolution?
   o Schooling?
   o Friends and family?
   o If there is a God why is there so much evil in the world?
   o Other

Parental upbringing

Some children are brought up to believe that there is no God and because we are shaped by our environment, it is possible that if you were brought up to believe that there is no God you will most likely accept this ideology without questioning it. However this doesn't make it true and we all owe it to ourselves to discover for ourselves whether or not God exists.

Science

Science mostly tries to refute the existence of God and this is encouraged by the theory of evolution which states that the world was created by a big bang and we human beings and animals and plants have come about as a result of thousands of years of evolution. They often use fossils to back their theory however they cannot explain how the big bang itself came about therefore this cannot be a valid reason to disprove the existence of God. And it is only a theory, it is not the truth therefore why deny the existence of God just because of a man-made theory?

Schooling

Our Western upbringing is based on rational thinking and teaches that only the things you can touch, smell, see, taste or hear are 'real' and valid because you can prove their existence. This is an error because there are many things that we believe but we cannot prove. Our emotions are very real to us however we cannot prove it. We all dream however we cannot prove it. We believe that the wind exist however who has ever seen the wind? We see the effect however we don't see the wind itself.

Friends and Family

Just like parental upbringing, some people are surrounded by friends and family who are all unbelievers. In this case it is difficult for the individual to believe in the existence of a God when no one else around them is a believer. However this is not a valid reason to disprove the existence of God. We are all individuals and we owe it to ourselves to ask whether or not there is a God and to search for the answers ourselves. As Socrates once stated "The unexamined life is not worth living". Take this opportunity to search whether or not there is a God.

If there is a God why is there so much evil in the world?
This is the one that gets a lot of people. They wrongfully believe that a good God would not allow evil to exist in the world. This is the ideal situation however when God made human beings, He gave us a choice and the first human beings who ever lived on the earth, Adam and Eve, made the choice that brought evil into the world when they decided to listen to the devil rather than to God. Freedom of choice means that we can choose to believe that there is a God and come to Him through His Holy Son Jesus Christ who lived on earth but never sinned and died to forgive us of our sins, or we can choose to ignore God and face the punishment of being separated from His love and protection for all eternity, the choice belongs to you.

Other
Please write down any other reason why you believe there is no God, then examine it to see whether or not it is based on prejudice of some kind.

3. **How do I know if God is real**?
If you are still unsure about the existence of God, there are simple steps that you can take to prove or disprove His existence. Follow these steps one-by-one and then judge for yourself, whether or not God exists:

1. Pray and ask God to prove to you that He exists. Say something like this 'Dear God, I want to believe in You. If you exist, please prove it to me'.
2. Take a Bible and read the fourth book in the New Testament called John. You can also download the Bible at www.biblegateway.com
3. Believe that Jesus Christ died to forgive you of your sins:

    "For all have sinned and fall short of the glory of God" (Romans 3:23)

    "For God so loved the world that He gave His only begotten Son, that whoever believes in Him should not perish but have everlasting life" (John 3:16)

4. Repent or turn back on your sins and make a choice not to do them anymore:

If we confess our sins, He is faithful and just to forgive us our sins and to cleanse us from all unrighteousness. If we say that we have not sinned, we make Him a liar, and His word is not in us (1 John 1:9-10)

5. Invite Jesus Christ into your heart:

That if you confess with your mouth the Lord Jesus and believe in your heart that God has raised Him from the dead, you will be saved (Romans 10:9)

To do this, you can pray a prayer like this:

Prayer of Surrender
Please take some time out and pray this prayer from your heart:

Lord Jesus, I believe You are the Son of God. I believe that You are the way, the truth and the life and no man comes to the Father but by You. I believe You died on the cross and You were raised from the dead.

I accept that I am a sinner and have come short of the glory of God. I now confess my sins and ask You to please forgive me for the sins of (........please take your time and name them one by one and make a decision not to do them again).

Please wash me clean with Your precious blood that was shed for me on the Cross. Please remove me from the kingdom of darkness and bring me into Your Kingdom of Light. I want to know you Jesus, and have a loving relationship with God my Father.

Please become the Lord of my life and fill me with Your Holy Spirit so that I can live a victorious life.

From today, please gain control over my spirit, my soul, my mind, my will and my emotions. Please help me to live for You. Thank You Jesus.

Father, I now come to You in the name of Jesus. Thank You for giving Jesus Christ Your Son to die for me so that I can have a loving relationship with You. Please fill me with Your Holy Spirit and guide and direct my steps from this day forward in Jesus name.

Father, I know You created me for a purpose. Please show me why You have created me and what You want me to do in Jesus' name.

Next Steps
Dear Friend, if you have prayed this prayer from your heart, you have become a child of God. Please get a Bible and start reading the Word of God, because the Word of God is Spirit and it is life. You literally become transformed as you read the Word of God.

I want to encourage you to be strong and depend on Jesus. You see, Satan, who is the prince of this world and the enemy of God, hates the children of God and he will therefore try to come against you to discourage you from following Jesus. But just know you will overcome all challenges that comes to you through Jesus Christ our Lord. Please find a Church where the pure Word of God is preached and join fellowship with other believers. This will help you to be strong and to grow in the Lord.

Dear Brother or Sister, if you have prayed this prayer, we would love to hear from you. Please write to us, and we will send you a Bible and some excellent reading material to help you on this Christian journey.

Please write to:
Latter-Rain Outpouring Revival Ministries
50 Copleston Road, Peckham
London
SE15 4AD
United Kingdom

4. Do you believe in God now?
Yes – continue to 30-day challenge
Still sceptical? – look at nature. Give yourself a week and go out every day and just look up at the sky and ask God to reveal Himself to you:

The heavens declare the glory of God; the skies proclaim the work of his hands
(Psalm 19:1)

5. Do you believe in God now?
Yes – proceed to the 30-day challenge

No – please pray and ask God to give you wisdom and revelation in the knowledge of Him.

Pray this prayer morning and evening for the next 30-days:

Prayer for Spiritual Wisdom
I pray that the God of our Lord Jesus Christ, the Father of glory, may give to me the Spirit of wisdom and revelation in the knowledge of Him, the eyes of my understanding being enlightened; that I may know what is the hope of His calling, what are the riches of the glory of His inheritance in the saints, and what is the exceeding greatness of His power toward us who believe, according to the working of His mighty power which He worked in Christ when He raised Him from the dead and seated Him at His right hand in the heavenly places, far above all principality and power and might and dominion, and every name that is named, not only in this age but also in that which is to come.

And He put all things under His feet, and gave Him to be head over all things to the church, which is His body, the fullness of Him who fills all in all.
(Ephesians 1:17-23)

30 Day challenge

You can only discover your purpose in God your Creator therefore now that you are a believer, you are ready for the 30-day Challenge.

For the next 30 days ask God to show you the purpose for your life. During this period please meditate on the scriptures that pertains to purpose and record any dreams, thoughts or ideas, prophecy, impressions that come to you.

How does God speak to us about our purpose?

There are many ways in which God, through His Holy Spirit may speak to us:

The Word
The Bible is the Word of God which will never change. Heaven and earth may pass away but the Word of God will never pass away. The Word of God is described as a Lamb for our feet and a Light for our path (Psalm 119:105). Light gives illumination where there is darkness therefore anytime we find ourselves in darkness and need advice about a particular situation we can turn to the Word of God for guidance.

Still small voice
When the Prophet Elijah was afraid and was running for his life from Jezebel, God spoke to him through a still small voice and told him who to anoint as King over Israel and who to anoint as his successor (1 Kings 19:12-16). The Holy Spirit does not shout, He often speaks to us through a gentle quiet voice which we hear through our spirit.

Audible voice
Sometimes God may speak to us through an audible voice. When Saul was going to the city of Damascus with a letter from the High Priest to find followers of The Lord to arrest and bring back to Jerusalem, a very bright light from heaven suddenly shined around him. He fell to the ground and heard a voice saying to him, "Saul, Saul! Why are you persecuting Me?" Saul said, "Who are you, Lord?" The voice answered, "I am Jesus, the One you are persecuting. Get up now and go into the city. Someone there will tell you what you must do."

The men traveling with Saul just stood there, unable to speak. They heard the voice, but they saw no one. Saul was blinded by this experience and after fasting for three days a follower of Jesus named Ananias came and laid hands on him so that he could see again. Saul then got baptised and he began to go to the synagogues to tell people about Jesus (Acts 9:1-22).

Dreams
The Bible is filled with numerous stories of men and women who have received guidance, warning, and advice through dreams. When the wise men left after seeing Baby Jesus, an Angel from the Lord came to Joseph in a dream. The Angel told him to get up and take the Child with His mother and escape to Egypt because Herod wanted to kill the Child. They were to stay in Egypt until the Angel told them to come back. When Herod died, an Angel from the Lord came to Joseph in a dream and said,

"Get up! Take the Child with His mother and go to Israel. Those who were trying to kill the Child are now dead" (Matthew 2:13-21).

Visions

A vision is a spiritual or mental image. Cornelius who was a Roman army officer had a vision in which he saw an Angel. The Angel told him that God had heard his prayers and had seen all his gifts to the poor and he was to send some men to the city of Joppa to get a man named Simon, who is also called Peter.

The next day Peter was going up to the roof to pray. He was hungry and wanted to eat but while they were preparing the food for Peter to eat, he also had a vision. He saw something coming down through the open sky. It looked like a big sheet being lowered to the ground by its four corners. In it were all kinds of animals, reptiles, and birds. Then a voice said to him, "Get up, Peter; kill anything here and eat it."

But Peter said, "I can't do that, Lord! I have never eaten anything that is not pure or fit to be used for food." But the voice said to him again, "God has made these things pure. Don't say they are unfit to eat." This happened three times. Then the whole thing was taken back up into heaven. When the vision was over the men that Cornelius sent had arrived and were waiting for him. As a result of his vision, Peter went to Cornelius house and Cornelius and all his household became believers in Jesus Christ and were the first Gentles to be filled with the Holy Spirit (Acts 10).

Prophecies

Prophecy is predicting the future with certainty as the Lord reveals it. God may at times speak to us through His messengers about things to come. Agabus was one such Prophet. He spoke with the help of the Spirit and said that a famine was coming to the whole world where there will be no food for people to eat. The Lord's followers decided that they would each send as much as they could to help their brothers and sisters who lived in Judea. They gathered the money and gave it to Barnabas and Saul, who took it to the elders in Judea (Acts 11:27-30).

Inner knowing

Inner knowing is the ability to know something through our spirit or heart. Human beings are spirits, we have a soul and live in a body. God does not look at our outward appearance but He looks at the heart and it is through our heart that His Spirit communicates to us "The Spirit Himself bears witness with our spirit that we are children of God." (Romans 8:16).

Scripture to meditate:

But I have raised you up for this very purpose, that I might show you my power and that my name might be proclaimed in all the earth (Exodus 9:16 - NIV)

Prayer:

Father I thank You that you have a purpose for everyone, including me. I know that You have raised me up to show Your power and that Your name might be proclaimed through all the earth.

Journal:

The Word (i.e. Bible, Preaching)

....
....
....
....
....
....
....

Still small voice

....
....
....
....
....
....
....

Audible voice

....
....
....
....
....
....
....

Dreams

....
....
....
....

....
....
....

Visions

....
....
....
....
....
....
....

Prophecies

....
....
....
....
....
....
....

Inner knowing

....
....
....
....
....
....
....

Day 2

Scriptures to meditate:

I know that you can do all things; no purpose of Yours can be thwarted (Job 42:2 - NIV).

Prayer:

Dear Lord, I know that You can do all things. Your purpose for my life can never be changed or stopped in Jesus name.

Journal:

The Word (i.e. Bible, Preaching)

....
....
....
....
....
....
....

Still small voice

....
....
....
....
....
....
....

Audible voice

....
....
....
....
....
....
....

Dreams

....
....
....
....
....
....
....

Visions

....
....
....
....
....
....
....

Prophecies

....
....
....
....
....
....
....

Inner knowing

....
....
....
....
....
....
....

Day 3

Many are the plans in a person's heart, but it is the Lord's purpose that prevails (Proverbs 19:21- NIV)

Prayer:
Yes Lord, I pray that every plan in my heart will align with Your plan and let Your purpose prevail in my life in Jesus name, amen.

Journal:

The Word (i.e. Bible, Preaching)

....
....
....
....
....
....
....

Still small voice

....
....
....
....
....
....
....

Audible voice

....
....
....
....
....
....
....

Dreams

....
....
....
....
....
....
....

Visions

....
....
....
....
....
....
....

Prophecies

....
....
....
....
....
....
....

Inner knowing

....
....
....
....
....
....
....

Scriptures to meditate:
The purposes of a person's heart are deep waters, but one who has insight draws them out (Proverbs 20:5 – NIV)

Prayer:
Dear Lord, I realise that the purpose You have for my life is already deep inside me. Please help me to discover it in Jesus name, amen.

Journal:

The Word (i.e. Bible, Preaching)

....
....
....
....
....
....
....

Still small voice

....
....
....
....
....
....
....

Audible voice

....
....
....
....
....
....
....

Dreams

....
....
....
....
....
....
....

Visions

....
....
....
....
....
....
....

Prophecies

....
....
....
....
....
....
....

Inner knowing

....
....
....
....
....
....
....

Day 5

Scriptures to meditate:
Therefore, my dear friends, as you have always obeyed—not only in my presence, but now much more in my absence—continue to work out your salvation with fear and trembling, for it is God who works in you to will and to act in order to fulfil His good purpose" (Philippians 2:12-13 - NIV)

Prayer:
Father, please work in me and let Your will be done in order to fulfil Your good purpose in my life in Jesus name.

Journal:

The Word (i.e. Bible, Preaching)

....
....
....
....
....
....
....

Still small voice

....
....
....
....
....
....
....

Audible voice

....
....
....
....
....
....
....

Dreams

....
....
....
....
....
....
....

Visions

....
....
....
....
....
....
....

Prophecies

....
....
....
....
....
....
....

Inner knowing

....
....
....
....
....
....
....

Day 6

Scriptures to meditate:
And we know that in all things God works for the good of those who love Him, who have been called according to His purpose (Romans 8:28 – NIV)

Prayer
Father, I thank You that all things are working together for good for me because I love You, and because I have been called according to Your purpose.

Journal:

The Word (i.e. Bible, Preaching)
....
....
....
....
....
....
....

Still small voice
....
....
....
....
....
....
....

Audible voice
....
....
....
....
....
....
....

Dreams
....
....
....
....
....
....
....

Visions

....
....
....
....
....
....
....

Prophecies

....
....
....
....
....
....
....

Inner knowing

....
....
....
....
....
....
....

Day 7

Scripture to meditate:
He has saved us and called us to a holy life—not because of anything we have done but because of His own purpose and grace (2 Timothy 1:9 – NIV)

Prayer
Father I thank You that You have saved me and called me to a holy life, not because of anything I have done, but because of Your own purpose and grace.

Journal:

The Word (i.e. Bible, Preaching)

....
....
....
....
....
....
....

Still small voice

....
....
....
....
....
....
....

Audible voice

....
....
....
....
....
....
....

Dreams

....
....
....
....
....
....
....

Visions

....
....
....
....
....
....
....

Prophecies

....
....
....
....
....
....
....

Inner knowing

....
....
....
....
....
....
....

Scriptures to meditate:

For God speaketh once, yea twice, yet man perceiveth it not. In a dream, in a vision of the night, when deep sleep falleth upon men, in slumberings upon the bed; Then He openeth the ears of men, and sealeth their instruction, That He may withdraw man from his purpose, and hide pride from man (Job 33:14-17 – KJV)

Prayer:

Father, I pray that as I sleep You would speak to me in a dream, open my ears and seal Your instructions in my heart and show me why You have created me in Jesus name, amen.

Journal:

The Word (i.e. Bible, Preaching)

....
....
....
....
....
....
....

Still small voice

....
....
....
....
....
....
....

Audible voice

....
....
....
....
....
....
....

Dreams

....
....
....
....
....

....
....

Visions

....
....
....
....
....
....
....

Prophecies

....
....
....
....
....
....
....

Inner knowing

....
....
....
....
....
....
....

Scriptures to meditate:

Without counsel purposes are disappointed: but in the multitude of counsellors they are established (Proverbs 15:22 – KJV)

Prayer:

Dear Lord, Your Word says that without counsellors purposes can be disappointed, but purposes are established in the multitude of counsellors. Please give me Godly counsellors who can help me to achieve the purpose You have for my life in Jesus name, amen.

Journal:

The Word (i.e. Bible, Preaching)

....
....
....
....
....
....
....

Still small voice

....
....
....
....
....
....
....

Audible voice

....
....
....
....
....
....
....

Dreams

....
....
....
....
....
....
....

Visions

....
....
....
....
....
....
....

Prophecies

....
....
....
....
....
....
....

Inner knowing

....
....
....
....
....
....
....

Day 10

Scriptures to meditate:
Every purpose is established by counsel: and with good advice make war (Proverbs 20:18)

Prayer:
Yes Lord, Your Word says that every purpose is established by counsel. Please give me good advisers who will help me to fight the good fight of faith in Jesus name, amen.

Journal:

The Word (i.e. Bible, Preaching)

....
....
....
....
....
....
....

Still small voice

....
....
....
....
....
....
....

Audible voice

....
....
....
....
....
....
....

Dreams

....
....
....
....
....
....
....

Visions

....
....
....
....
....
....
....

Prophecies

....
....
....
....
....
....
....

Inner knowing

....
....
....
....
....
....
....

Day 11

Scriptures to meditate:

To everything there is a season, and a time to every purpose under the heaven (Ecclesiastes 3:1)

Prayer:

Dear Lord, I thank You that there is a season for everything. Please let Your purpose for my life come forth at the right season and time in Jesus name, amen.

Journal:

The Word (i.e. Bible, Preaching)

....
....
....
....
....
....
....

Still small voice

....
....
....
....
....
....
....

Audible voice

....
....
....
....
....
....
....

Dreams

....
....
....
....
....
....
....

Visions

....
....
....
....
....
....
....

Prophecies

....
....
....
....
....
....
....

Inner knowing

....
....
....
....
....
....
....

Scriptures to meditate:

I said in mine heart, God shall judge the righteous and the wicked: for there is a time there for every purpose and for every work (Ecclesiastes 3:17)

Prayer

Lord I thank You that there is a time for every purpose and for every work. Please reveal the time for my purpose to me in Jesus name, amen.

Journal:

The Word (i.e. Bible, Preaching)

....
....
....
....
....
....
....

Still small voice

....
....
....
....
....
....
....

Audible voice

....
....
....
....
....
....
....

Dreams

....
....
....
....
....
....
....

Visions

....
....
....
....
....
....
....

Prophecies

....
....
....
....
....
....
....

Inner knowing

....
....
....
....
....
....
....

Day 13

Scriptures to mediate:

This is the purpose that is purposed upon the whole earth: and this is the hand that is stretched out upon all the nations.

For the Lord of hosts hath purposed, and who shall disannul it? and His hand is stretched out, and who shall turn it back? (Isaiah 14:26-27)

Prayer:

Lord I thank You that nobody can change Your purposes, and when You stretch out Your hand, nobody can turn it back. Please let Your purpose for my life be established in Jesus name, amen.

Journal:

The Word (i.e. Bible, Preaching)

....
....
....
....
....
....
....

Still small voice

....
....
....
....
....
....
....

Audible voice

....
....
....
....
....
....
....

Dreams

....
....
....
....
....

....
....

Visions

....
....
....
....
....
....
....

Prophecies

....
....
....
....
....
....
....

Inner knowing

....
....
....
....
....
....
....

Day 14

Scriptures to meditate:
Who, when he came, and had seen the grace of God, was glad, and exhorted them all, that with purpose of heart they would cleave unto the Lord (Acts 11:23)

Prayer:
Lord, please help me so that that the purpose of my heart will be to cleave to You in Jesus name, amen.

Journal:

The Word (i.e. Bible, Preaching)

....
....
....
....
....
....
....

Still small voice

....
....
....
....
....
....
....

Audible voice

....
....
....
....
....
....
....

Dreams

....
....
....
....
....
....
....

Visions

....
....
....
....
....
....
....

Prophecies

....
....
....
....
....
....
....

Inner knowing

....
....
....
....
....
....
....

Day 15

Scriptures to meditate:
But rise, and stand upon thy feet: for I have appeared unto thee for this purpose, to make thee a minister and a witness both of these things which thou hast seen, and of those things in the which I will appear unto thee (Acts 26:16)

Prayer:
Father, please let The Lord Jesus appear to me, as He appeared to Paul, to show me the purpose for my life so that I can be a minister and a witness both of the things which I have seen in Jesus name, amen.

Journal:

The Word (i.e. Bible, Preaching)
....
....
....
....
....
....
....

Still small voice
....
....
....
....
....
....
....

Audible voice
....
....
....
....
....
....
....

Dreams
....
....
....
....
....
....
....

Visions

....
....
....
....
....
....
....

Prophecies

....
....
....
....
....
....
....

Inner knowing

....
....
....
....
....
....
....

Scriptures to meditate:

For the children being not yet born, neither having done any good or evil, that the purpose of God according to election might stand, not of works, but of him that calleth (Romans 9:11)

Prayer:

Dear Lord, please let Your purpose for calling and electing me stand in Jesus name, amen.

Journal:

The Word (i.e. Bible, Preaching)

....
....
....
....
....
....
....

Still small voice

....
....
....
....
....
....
....

Audible voice

....
....
....
....
....
....
....

Dreams

....
....
....
....
....
....
....

Visions

....
....
....
....
....
....
....

Prophecies

....
....
....
....
....
....
....

Inner knowing

....
....
....
....
....
....
....

Scriptures to meditate:
For the scripture saith unto Pharaoh, Even for this same purpose have I raised thee up, that I might shew my power in thee, and that my name might be declared throughout all the earth (Romans 9:17)

Prayer:
Dear Lord, as You raised up Pharaoh, so please raise me up to show your power in me, and that Your name might be declared throughout the earth in Jesus name, amen.

Journal:

The Word (i.e. Bible, Preaching)

....
....
....
....
....
....
....

Still small voice

....
....
....
....
....
....
....

Audible voice

....
....
....
....
....
....
....

Dreams

....
....
....
....
....
....
....

Visions

....
....
....
....
....
....
....

Prophecies

....
....
....
....
....
....
....

Inner knowing

....
....
....
....
....
....
....

Scriptures to meditate:

In whom also we have obtained an inheritance, being predestinated according to the purpose of him who worketh all things after the counsel of his own will (Ephesians 1:11)

Prayer:

Lord, I thank You that I have been predestined according to Your purpose and Your own will in Jesus name.

Journal:

The Word (i.e. Bible, Preaching)

....
....
....
....
....
....
....

Still small voice

....
....
....
....
....
....
....

Audible voice

....
....
....
....
....
....
....

Dreams

....
....
....
....
....
....
....

Visions

....
....
....
....
....
....
....

Prophecies

....
....
....
....
....
....
....

Inner knowing

....
....
....
....
....
....
....

Scriptures to meditate:
According to the eternal purpose which he purposed in Christ Jesus our Lord (Ephesians 3:11)

Prayer:
Father, please show me Your eternal purpose for my life which You purposed in Christ Jesus our Lord.

Journal:

The Word (i.e. Bible, Preaching)

....
....
....
....
....
....
....

Still small voice

....
....
....
....
....
....
....

Audible voice

....
....
....
....
....
....
....

Dreams

....
....
....
....
....
....
....

Visions

....
....
....
....
....
....
....

Prophecies

....
....
....
....
....
....
....

Inner knowing

....
....
....
....
....
....
....

Day 20

Scriptures to meditate:
Whom I have sent unto you for the same purpose, that ye might know our affairs, and that he might comfort your hearts (Ephesians 6:22)

Prayer:
Lord, I pray that You will send me the destiny partners who will help me to fulfil Your purpose for my life in Jesus name, amen.

Journal:

The Word (i.e. Bible, Preaching)

....
....
....
....
....
....
....

Still small voice

....
....
....
....
....
....
....

Audible voice

....
....
....
....
....
....
....

Dreams

....
....
....
....
....
....
....

Visions

....
....
....
....
....
....
....

Prophecies

....
....
....
....
....
....
....

Inner knowing

....
....
....
....
....
....
....

Day 21

Scriptures to meditate:
But thou hast fully known my doctrine, manner of life, purpose, faith, longsuffering, charity, patience (2 Timothy 3:10)

Prayer:
Lord, please help me to be able to know and articulate my purpose to the world in Jesus name, amen.

Journal:

The Word (i.e. Bible, Preaching)

....
....
....
....
....
....
....

Still small voice

....
....
....
....
....
....
....

Audible voice

....
....
....
....
....
....
....

Dreams

....
....
....
....
....
....
....

Visions

....
....
....
....
....
....
....

Prophecies

....
....
....
....
....
....
....

Inner knowing

....
....
....
....
....
....
....

Scriptures to meditate:

He that committeth sin is of the devil; for the devil sinneth from the beginning. For this purpose the Son of God was manifested, that he might destroy the works of the devil (1 John 3:8)

Prayer:

Dear Lord, I thank You that the purpose of Jesus Christ was to destroy the works of the devil. Please let every works of the devil in my life be destroyed by the power in the Blood of Jesus, in Jesus name, amen.

Journal:

The Word (i.e. Bible, Preaching)

....
....
....
....
....
....
....

Still small voice

....
....
....
....
....
....
....

Audible voice

....
....
....
....
....
....
....

Dreams

....
....
....
....
....
....
....

Visions

....
....
....
....
....
....
....

Prophecies

....
....
....
....
....
....
....

Inner knowing

....
....
....
....
....
....

Scriptures to meditate:
But He said to them, "I must preach the kingdom of God to the other cities also, because for this purpose I have been sent." And He was preaching in the synagogues of Galilee (Luke 4:44 NKJV)

Prayer:
Dear Lord, please help me to know my purpose in life just like Jesus knew His purpose in Jesus name, amen.

Journal:

The Word (i.e. Bible, Preaching)

....
....
....
....
....
....
....

Still small voice

....
....
....
....
....
....
....

Audible voice

....
....
....
....
....
....
....

Dreams

....
....
....
....
....
....
....

Visions

....
....
....
....
....
....
....

Prophecies

....
....
....
....
....
....
....

Inner knowing

....
....
....
....
....
....
....

Scriptures to mediate:
When I therefore was thus minded, did I use lightness? or the things that I purpose, do I purpose according to the flesh, that with me there should be yea yea, and nay nay?
(2 Corinthians 1:17)

Prayer:
Dear Lord, please let my purpose be according to the Spirit and not to the flesh because Your word tells me that they that sow to the flesh shall reap corruption but they that sow to the Spirit shall reap life everlasting (Galatians 6:8) in Jesus name.

Journal:

The Word (i.e. Bible, Preaching)
....
....
....
....
....
....
....

Still small voice
....
....
....
....
....
....
....

Audible voice
....
....
....
....
....
....
....

Dreams
....
....
....
....
....

....
....

Visions

....
....
....
....
....
....
....

Prophecies

....
....
....
....
....
....
....

Inner knowing

....
....
....
....
....
....
....

Scriptures to meditate:
And when the south wind blew softly, supposing that they had obtained their purpose, loosing thence, they sailed close by Crete (Acts 27:13)

Prayer:
Dear Lord, please don't let any wind, storm, fire, flood or any adversities in life prevent me from obtaining my purpose in Jesus name, amen.

Journal:

The Word (i.e. Bible, Preaching)

....
....
....
....
....
....
....

Still small voice

....
....
....
....
....
....
....

Audible voice

....
....
....
....
....
....
....

Dreams

....
....
....
....
....
....
....

Visions

....
....
....
....
....
....
....

Prophecies

....
....
....
....
....
....
....

Inner knowing

....
....
....
....
....
....
....

Day 26

Scriptures to meditate:
But the centurion, willing to save Paul, kept them from their purpose; and commanded that they which could swim should cast themselves first into the sea, and get to land (Acts 27:43)

Prayer:
Dear Lord, just like You sent the centurion to save Paul and keep the soldiers from their purpose of harming Paul, so please send helpers who will help me in my hour of need so that no harm will come to me in Jesus name, amen.

Journal:

The Word (i.e. Bible, Preaching)
....
....
....
....
....
....
....

Still small voice
....
....
....
....
....
....
....

Audible voice
....
....
....
....
....
....
....

Dreams
....
....
....
....
....

....
....

Visions

....
....
....
....
....
....
....

Prophecies

....
....
....
....
....
....
....

Inner knowing

....
....
....
....
....
....
....

Scriptures to meditate:
The Lord of hosts hath sworn, saying, Surely as I have thought, so shall it come to pass; and as I have purposed, so shall it stand (Isaiah 14:24)

Prayer:
Father, I thank You that whatever purpose You have for my life shall come to pass and it shall stand in Jesus name.

Journal:

The Word (i.e. Bible, Preaching)
....
....
....
....
....
....
....

Still small voice
....
....
....
....
....
....
....

Audible voice

....
....
....
....
....
....
....

Dreams

....
....
....
....
....
....
....

Visions

....
....
....
....
....
....
....

Prophecies

....
....
....
....
....
....
....

Inner knowing

....
....
....
....
....
....
....

Day 28

Scriptures to meditate:
So God created man in his own image, in the image of God created he him; male and female created he them. And God blessed them, and God said unto them, Be fruitful, and multiply, and replenish the earth, and subdue it: and have dominion over the fish of the sea, and over the fowl of the air, and over every living thing that moveth upon the earth (Genesis 1:28)

Prayer:
Father, I thank You for creating me in Your own image. Thank that You have blessed me. Please help me to be fruitful, and multiply, and replenish the earth, and subdue it, and have dominion over the fish of the sea, and over the fowl of the air, and over every living that that moveth upon the earth in Jesus name, amen.

Journal:

The Word (i.e. Bible, Preaching)

....
....
....
....
....
....
....

Still small voice

....
....
....
....
....
....
....

Audible voice

....
....
....
....
....
....
....

Dreams

....
....
....
....

....
....
....

Visions

....
....
....
....
....
....
....

Prophecies

....
....
....
....
....
....
....

Inner knowing

....
....
....
....
....
....
....

Scriptures to meditate

For I know the thoughts that I think toward you, saith the Lord, thoughts of peace, and not of evil, to give you an expected end (Jeremiah 29:11)

Prayer:

Dear Lord, I thank You that You know the thoughts that You think towards me. I thank You that they are thoughts of peace, and not of evil, to give me an expected end in Jesus name.

Journal:

The Word (i.e. Bible, Preaching)

....
....
....
....
....
....
....

Still small voice

....
....
....
....
....
....
....

Audible voice

....
....
....
....
....
....
....

Dreams

....
....
....
....
....
....
....

Visions

....
....
....
....
....
....
....

Prophecies

....
....
....
....
....
....
....

Inner knowing

....
....
....
....
....
....
....

Scriptures to meditate:
Let us hear the conclusion of the whole matter: Fear God, and keep his commandments: for this is the whole duty of man (Ecclesiastes 12:13)

Prayer:
Dear Lord, I thank You for bringing me to the last day of my 30-day purpose challenge. Lord, I accept the conclusion of the whole matter. Please help me to fear You, and keep Your commandments, for this is the whole duty of man in Jesus name, amen.

Journal:

The Word (i.e. Bible, Preaching)
....
....
....
....
....
....
....

Still small voice
....
....
....
....
....
....
....

Audible voice
....
....
....
....
....
....
....

Dreams
....
....
....
....
....
....
....

Visions

....
....
....
....
....
....
....

Prophecies

....
....
....
....
....
....
....

Inner knowing

....
....
....
....
....
....
....

Follow-up action

Based on all the revelations you have received during the last 30 days, you should now follow the steps below to make these dreams, thoughts and ideas, prophecies and impressions become a reality:

1. **Write down your dreams / thoughts/ prophecies / impressions** that you have received which indicates your future path

2. **Acknowledge God**
Dreams / prophecies / thoughts / impressions and their meaning are given by God. Therefore, once you have written them down, acknowledge that it is God who gave them to you and thank Him for it

3. **Ask God for interpretation**
Now that you have acknowledged that it is God that gave you the dreams, impressions, prophecies, ideas etc. ask God to tell you what they mean. He is the one who gave them to You therefore He is your best guide to understanding them. To do this I suggest you simply go humbly to God and ask Him what they mean. Do this every night for 30 days before you sleep until the answer comes to you. You simply say something like this:

Father God, please tell me, what does these dreams mean?
What does these prophecies mean?
What does these thoughts and ideas, mean?
What does these impressions mean?

4. **Keep a record of the answers**
For the duration of that 30 days, have a notebook and pen next to your bed, in your pocket or handbag when you go out so that if an answer or anything of significance comes to you while you sleep or you are out and about you can write it down. The meaning that you seek may come in a day, two weeks, or it may take the full 30 days; don't give up, it will come. Sometimes the answers may come to you as a vision or a thought when you are awake, perhaps doing something mundane such as washing dishes.

5. **Think of ideas of how to achieve the dream**
Next, take a clean sheet of paper and ask yourself this question:

Based on the answers I got about the dreams, prophecies, ideas and impressions how can it be achieved?

Write down any thoughts or ideas that come to mind, for example, if your purpose to be an author and change the world through your books, sit down with a notepad and ask God, "what topic would You want me to write about? Fiction, Non-Fiction?" As you sit still, answers will come to you, possible book titles will form. Write these down as they come, along with anything else that manifests from your brainstorming. Try to keep at it until at least 20 ideas are on your list. You may do this exercise and find that inspiration comes to you much later when you are in the middle of something else.

6. Commit your ideas to God

Once you have your great ideas written down, commit them into the hands of God and ask Him for guidance and wisdom on the best way to move forward:

Commit your way to the Lord,
Trust also in Him,
And He shall bring it to pass.
Psalm 37:5

Commit your works to the Lord,
And your thoughts will be established.
Proverbs 16:3

7. Take action

Next look at the list of ideas and consider what you can take action on immediately and do it. Look at this list every morning for the next 30 days and add more ideas to it as they come. Do something every day that moves you towards the attainment of your purpose. You will be astounded by what you achieve in a short space of time. To help you to track your progress, do record your achievements on a daily basis. Remember to keep praying to God for courage and strength to take these steps.

Next Steps

Once you have taken the above steps then you are ready for the next two:

1. Seek a Coach / Mentor / Adviser – a journey of two years can be shortened to 2 months with the right guidance and advice from a coach or mentor. A coach can be an author or someone who has already achieved what you are trying to achieve. Blessing Spiritual Life Coaching exists to help people who want to discover their purpose and reach their full potential. Please contact us for your free consultation.
2. Review – review your purpose on a regular basis, ideally once a week, at the end of each month, every quarter and once a year to ensure that you are living a life of purpose and reaching your full potential.

What is my Purpose?

At the end of the 30-day challenge you should be much clearer about your purpose. Please write it down below. And don't forget this statement of purpose may change with experience and as new opportunities come your way. And remember that your purpose will always be about people and how you can better the lives of others.

At the end of the 30-day challenge, I believe that my purpose is to:

....
....
....
....
....
....
....

The statement of your purpose does not have to be a long sentence. For example it could be something like this:

"My purpose is to empower people to discover their purpose and reach their full potential"
"My purpose is to serve humanity creatively"
"My purpose is to bring up God-fearing children"
"My purpose is to make money so I can help the poor"
"My purpose is to be a blessing to the world"

There is nothing like waking up every day and living life on purpose. So now that you know your purpose, wake up and live and serve God and humanity.

Re-Discovering Your Identity

Based on the revelations received, can you now answer the following questions?

1. Who am I? (how would you describe yourself?)

....
....
....
....
....

2. What am I passionate about?

....
....
....
....
....

3. What am I naturally good at? (i.e. gifts and talents)

....
....
....
....
....

4. What would you like to do if I had all the time, skills and resources?

....
....
....
....

5. What would I like to change in the world if I could?

....
....
....
....
....

6. Why do I think I have created?

....
....
....
....
....

7. What would I like the world to remember me by?

....
....

Blessing Spiritual Life Coaching

About Blessing Spiritual Life Coaching
We offer bespoke spiritual life coaching services to people from all walks of life who want to discover their purpose and achieve their full potential.

What can Spiritual Coaching do for me?
Spiritual Life Coaching is for you if you want to:
•   Develop a relationship with God;
•   Live a life of meaning and fulfilment;
•   Make your dreams come true;
•   Take control of your life and live the life you desire;
•   Identify your gifts and talents and share them with the world;
•   Discover yourself and reach your full potential.

Contact Us:
Contact me and book your free consultation today:

Email: info@blessingcoaching.com
Tel: +44(0)7984616693
Website: www.blessingcoaching.com

About the Author

Blessing is a Speaker, Teacher and Coach, who is passionate about purpose and desires to see everyone fulfil their purpose and reach their full potential.

Blessing is currently studying Theology at the London School of Theology and she also has a degree in Philosophy and Politics from Exeter University and a Master's degree in Development Studies from the School of Oriental and African Studies, London.

She has a wealth of international experience from governmental and educational institutions, having worked at the Commonwealth Secretariat, Charity Commission and City University London.

In her leisure-time Blessing loves to read and enjoys going on long walks with her husband.

Blessing is married and lives in London, UK.